This book belongs to

Age

Favourite player

Prediction of Ipswich Town's final position this season

Prediction of Sky Bet Championship winners this season

Prediction of FA Cup winners this season

Prediction of Capital One Cup winners this season

Prediction of teams to be relegated from the Sky Bet Championship this season:

22nd

23rd

24th

Written by twocan

Contributors:
Lee Hyde & Rob Mason

A TWOCAN PUBLICATION

Every effort has been made to ensure the accuracy of information within this publication but the publishers cannot be held responsible for any errors or omissions.

Views expressed are those of the author and do not necessarily represent those of the publishers or the football club.

ISBN 978-1-909872-42-4

PICTURE CREDITS

Action Images,
Press Association,
Dan Sakal & Warren Page

£7.99

adidas
marcus
evans

CONTENTS

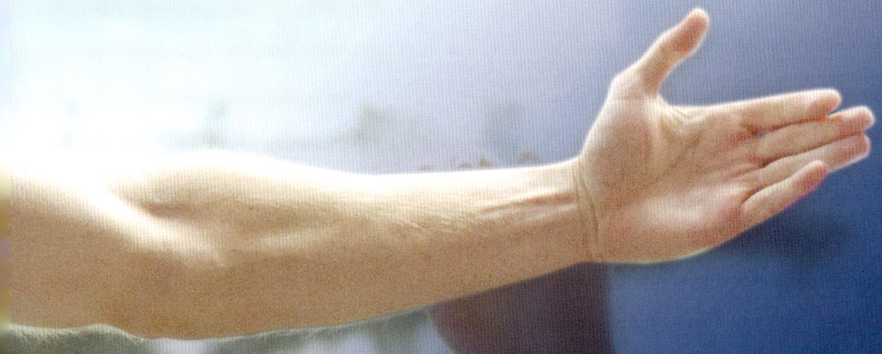

THE TEAM 2015/16

Back Row: Brett Pitman, Luke Chambers (capt), Christophe Berra, Bartosz Bialkowski, Dean Gerken, Tommy Smith, Daryl Murphy, Cole Skuse.

Middle Row: Ken Goody (Kit Management Dept.), Matt Byard (Head Physio), Dick Parker (Kit Management Dept.), Malcolm Webster (Goalkeeping Coach), Jonathan Parr, Teddy Bishop, David McGoldrick, Kevin Bru, Luke Hyam, Ainsley Maitland-Niles, Mark Kennedy (U21's Manager), James Pullen (Kit Manager), Alex Chapman (Physio).

Front Row: Jordan Miles (Performance Analyst), Ryan Fraser, Freddie Sears, Dave Bowman (Director of Football), Mick McCarthy (Manager), Terry Connor (Assistant Manager), Jay Tabb, Alex Henshall, Andy Liddell (Fitness Coach).

JONATHAN PARR 02

Position: Defender **Nationality:** Norwegian
DOB: 21.10.88

A solid defender, Parr joined Blues in the summer of 2014. He operates predominately as a left-back but can play in a number of positions. He has also represented Norway at full international level.

DEAN GERKEN 01

Position: Goalkeeper **Nationality:** English
DOB: 22.05.85

Gerken joined Ipswich in July 2013 after impressing manager Mick McCarthy whilst on trial. The stopper will again battle it out with Bartosz Bialkowski for the number one spot at Portman Road this term.

JONAS KNUDSEN 03

Position: Defender **Nationality:** Danish
DOB: 16.09.92

Knudsen joined Town on a three-year deal this summer. He has already made over 100 domestic appearances for Danish Superliga side Esbjerg and is well known for his long throw-in which the Blues will look to utilise this season.

THE SQUAD 2015/16

TOMMY SMITH 05

Position: Defender **Nationality:** New Zealander
DOB: 31.03.90

A product of the Blues Academy, Smith has made over 200 appearances for the club and is always a goal threat from set pieces. Internationally, he has represented New Zealand on a number of occasions.

LUKE CHAMBERS 04

Position: Defender **Nationality:** English
DOB: 28.09.85

Chambers joined Ipswich Town on a free transfer in July 2012 and has since become a firm fans' favourite. He has remained Club captain again this season and is set to surpass 150 league appearances for the Blues this term.

CHRISTOPHE BERRA 06

Position: Defender **Nationality:** Scottish
DOB: 31.01.85

Berra signed for Ipswich Town in July 2013 as a free agent and was named Player of the Season in his first campaign at Portman Road. He has also represented Scotland internationally a number of times.

AINSLEY MAITLAND-NILES 07

Position: Midfielder **Nationality:** English
DOB: 29.08.97

Maitland-Niles joined Town on a season-long loan from Arsenal. He has featured for the Gunners in the Champions League and the Premier League and will now be looking to gain further first-team experience at Portman Road.

COLE SKUSE 08

Position: Midfielder **Nationality:** English
DOB: 29.03.86

Skuse joined Ipswich Town in 2013 from Bristol City, where he had spent his entire career. Although naturally a central midfielder, he can also fill in at right-back and adds experience and steel to the Town ranks.

DARYL MURPHY 09

Position: Striker **Nationality:** Irish
DOB: 15.03.83

Murphy went into this season on the back of an amazing term, leading the Championship scoring charts with 27 goals as well as being named Town's Player of the Year. He signed a new contract with the Blues to remain at Portman Rd until 2017.

DAVID McGOLDRICK 10

Position: Striker **Nationality:** Irish
DOB: 29.11.87

A skilful frontman who possesses pace, McGoldrick signed a permanent deal with Ipswich in July 2013 after a successful loan spell. He received his first call up to the Republic of Ireland squad last season.

BRETT PITMAN 11

Position: Striker **Nationality:** English
DOB: 31.01.88

Pitman signed a three-year deal with the Blues in the summer, providing some serious competition up front. Since making his debut in 2006/07, he has scored over 100 league goals throughout the Football League.

JAMES ALABI 12

Position: Striker **Nationality:** English
DOB: 08.11.94

A powerful striker, Alabi moved to Town after a trial, following his release from Stoke City. He made an instant impact on his debut for Blues, scoring in the 4-1 Capital One Cup extra-time victory over Doncaster.

RYAN FRASER 14

Position: Midfielder **Nationality:** Scottish
DOB: 24.02.94

A rapid winger, Fraser joined Ipswich Town on loan from Bournemouth this summer. He hopes his time at the Blues can help push him into Scotland's first team, although he already has several caps for the U21 side.

TOMMY OAR 15

Position: Midfielder **Nationality:** Australian
DOB: 10.12.91

Oar joined Ipswich Town on a free transfer from FC Utrecht in August 2015, penning a two-year deal. He has over thirty caps for the Australian national team and participated in the 2014 FIFA World Cup.

GILES COKE 16

Position: Midfielder **Nationality:** English
DOB: 03.06.86

Coke signed a two-year contract with the Blues this summer following a successful trial period. He has worked his way up the Football League having begun his career at Isthmian Premier League side Kingstonian.

KEVIN BRU 17

Position: Midfielder **Nationality:** Mauritian
DOB: 12.12.88

A French-Mauritian midfielder, Bru joined Town on a free transfer in July 2014 after leaving Bulgarian side, Levski Sofia. He has played in France, Italy and Bulgaria and has been capped by Mauritius at international level.

JAY TABB 18

Position: Midfielder **Nationality:** Irish
DOB: 21.02.84

An experienced campaigner, Tabb completed a permanent switch to Town following a successful loan spell in the summer of 2013. He has had a taste of the international circuit, earning 10 caps for the Republic of Ireland U21s.

LUKE HYAM 19

Position: Midfielder **Nationality:** English
DOB: 24.10.91

An Ipswich-born midfielder, Hyam is a product of the Ipswich Town Academy. He adds energy and tenacity to the Blues midfield and is often deployed just in front of the defence, breaking up opposition attacks.

FREDDIE SEARS 20

Position: Striker **Nationality:** English
DOB: 27.11.89

Town added to their frontline in January 2015, with the permanent capture of Sears from Colchester. The former West Ham trainee signed a deal until 2017 and was Colchester's top scorer before moving to join the Blues.

PIOTR MALARCZYK 21

Position: Defender **Nationality:** Polish
DOB: 01.08.91

A strong defender who is capable of playing at either centre-half or right-back, Malarczyk joined Town for an undisclosed fee, moving from Polish side Korona Kielce where he'd made over 125 appearances and was captain.

ALEX HENSHALL 23

Position: Midfielder **Nationality:** English
DOB: 15.02.94

An exciting prospect, Henshall completed a permanent move to Portman Road following a loan spell in June 2014. He joined the Blues from Manchester City - who paid a six-figure sum to sign him as a 15-year-old.

JONATHAN DOUGLAS 22

Position: Midfielder **Nationality:** Irish
DOB: 22.11.81

Douglas signed for Town less than a week before the beginning of this season. He brings a wealth of experience to the squad and made his name as a tenacious midfielder whose work rate has always been a huge asset to his team.

DYLAN CONNOLLY 24

Position: Midfielder **Nationality:** Irish
DOB: 02.05.95

Connolly has been described as 'lightning quick' by a former manager and is thought of very highly at Portman Road. He signed from Shelbourne in February 2015 and is hoping to break into the Blues first-team.

ADAM McDONNELL 26

Position: Midfielder **Nationality:** Irish
DOB: 14.05.97

McDonnell joined Town from Shelbourne this summer and is highly regarded at Portman Road. He is likely to feature mainly for the U21s this term, although will be looking to break into Mick McCarthy's side.

JOSH YORWERTH 25

Position: Defender **Nationality:** Welsh
DOB: 01.01.95

Yorwerth signed for the Blues on a two-year deal from Cardiff City in the summer following an extended trial at Town. He failed to make a first-team appearance for the Welsh side but will look to hit the ground running with the Blues.

TEDDY BISHOP 27

Position: Midfielder **Nationality:** English
DOB: 15.07.96

Bishop is an Academy scholar who has progressed right through to the first-team, since joining Town as an eight year-old. He likes to get on the ball and link play from defence to attack.

JOSH EMMANUEL 29

Position: Defender **Nationality:** English
DOB: 18.08.97

Formerly of West Ham, Emmanuel has progressed through the Academy at Town and is highly regarded as one for the future. He recently penned a pro contract with the Blues, after impressing with his progress.

MYLES KENLOCK 30

Position: Defender **Nationality:** English
DOB: 29.11.96

Kenlock joined in 2014 as a scholar, following trials at several clubs including some in the Premier League. He impressed Mick McCarthy over pre-season and made his full debut in the Capital One Cup win over Stevenage.

BARTOSZ BIALKOWSKI 33

Position: Goalkeeper **Nationality:** Polish
DOB. 06.07.87

Bialkowski joined the Blues from Notts County in July 2014, signing a two-year deal at Portman Road. He actually spent time with the Blues on loan earlier in his career but never made an appearance in the first-team.

LARSEN TOURE 39

Position: Midfielder **Nationality:** Guinean
DOB: 20.07.84

A Guinean international, Toure joined the Town squad this August having left French side Arles-Avignon and will provide another attacking option. He has previously turned out for Lille and Brest in France as well as in Bulgaria with Levski Sofia.

Town went in to the second half of the season sitting top of the League (albeit only for an hour or so...) having emphatically defeated fellow promotion chasers Brentford at Griffin Park on Boxing Day, 4-2. This was followed up with a 3-0 home win over Charlton Athletic on 30th December to finish a memorable December, winning at home to Leeds United and Middlesbrough too with a draw on the road at Bolton Wanderers. Ipswich were on red-hot form having scored 13 goals and conceded only 3 during this period.

SECOND HALF OF THE SEASON

Having only lost three matches in the opening half of the season, Town would go on to struggle to replicate this form in the second half of the season, losing nine and drawing four of their last 22 games. January saw a defeat at home to early-season promotion favourites Derby County and away to Brighton & Hove Albion sandwich an away victory at struggling Millwall. Town played Wigan at home on the last day of the month, earning a 0-0 draw. The winter transfer window closed with Town having added Noel Hunt and Paddy Kenny on short-term deals with Freddie Sears and Dylan Connolly arriving on longer-term contracts. Freddie Veseli, Frank Nouble and Balint Bajner left the Club during this transfer window.

February saw further inconsistency, albeit with more positive results. An early defeat to Rotherham left Town slipping away from the automatic promotion places into fifth although by the end of the month the Blues' were back up to third with three wins out of four matches against Sheffield Wednesday, Fulham and Birmingham City. A rare home defeat to Reading was the only other blemish on the record for the month. Luke Varney (loan from Blackburn Rovers), Chris Wood (loan from Leicester City) and Richard Chaplow (loan from Millwall) were drafted in to the Town squad to add experience and depth.

A difficult March saw Town drop out of the top six for most parts, having occupied one of these positions since early-November. Defeats at Norwich City, Leeds United and Middlesbrough with a draw at home to Brentford looked to have put the brakes on Town's promotion bid, although recovering with two consecutive wins, at home to Bolton Wanderers and a stoppage time winner away to Watford boosted confidence ahead of the run-in.

With only seven matches remaining Town needed to consolidate their position in the Play-Offs with the chance of automatic promotion having all but disappeared. The pressure increased with the Blues drawing at home to Bournemouth and losing away at Huddersfield. Ipswich Town were down to eighth in the League. The next four games produced high drama - averaging 3.5 goals per game, fortunately Town came out fighting.

Two home victories in four days, 3-2 over Blackpool and 3-1 over Cardiff City, followed by a credible 1-1 draw at Play-Off hopefuls Wolverhampton Wanderers had Town back in the driving seat. The last home match of the regular season against Nottingham Forest needed to produce three points. Freddie Sears' 83rd minute winner almost tore the roof off Portman Road!

Town headed to Blackburn in fifth place knowing that a win would seal their Play-Off spot. It was a tense day for fans up and down the country. The game ebbed and flowed, with goals for both sides. Town scored an early goal through Daryl Murphy to settle fans nerves; however by the 58th minute Ipswich were behind 3-1. Fortunately other teams were feeling the pressure too. Derby were behind to Reading... 2-0. That was enough for Town. Brentford had sealed their place, finishing fifth with a 3-0 win at home to Wigan. Wolves, who had started the day in eighth, were chasing their Play-Off spot hard - a 4-2 win at home to Millwall almost nicked their place. Ipswich were awarded a late penalty which top scorer Daryl Murphy slotted home to reduce the margin of defeat to 3-2. At the same time Derby County conceded a third goal. Town could breathe a sigh of relief. A defeat in the rain at Blackburn has never been greeted with such a cheer. Ipswich Town had made the Play-Offs where they would meet their local rivals Norwich City.

The first-leg Play-Off semi-final was played in front of a full-house, and watching TV audience around the world, at Portman Road. A very credible 1-1 draw with Paul Anderson grabbing Town's goal set up an unbelievable 90-minute showdown at Carrow Road. At half-time in the second leg it was still all-square with the teams going in at 0-0. The second-half however produced further drama in this most incredible of seasons. An early foray into the Ipswich Town penalty area saw Christophe Berra receive a red-card for handling on the goal-line. The resulting penalty kick was scored by City's Wes Hoolahan. Town rallied... the ten men found strength and surged forward. A Tommy Smith goal on the hour gave hope to the packed away supporters' area. Sadly it wasn't to last with Nathan Redmond and Cameron Jerome scoring in the space of 12 minutes to seal a 3-1 victory for the hosts.

Ipswich Town had battled hard; they'd given it their all, not only in this match but for the whole season. It was a tremendous season of growth as a squad and a fantastic platform from which to build upon. The positivity quickly overshadowed the disappointment of coming so close with fans excitedly anticipating what the 2015/16 season would bring.

There are too many balls in these action shots!
Can you figure out which balls are real?

WHAT BALL?

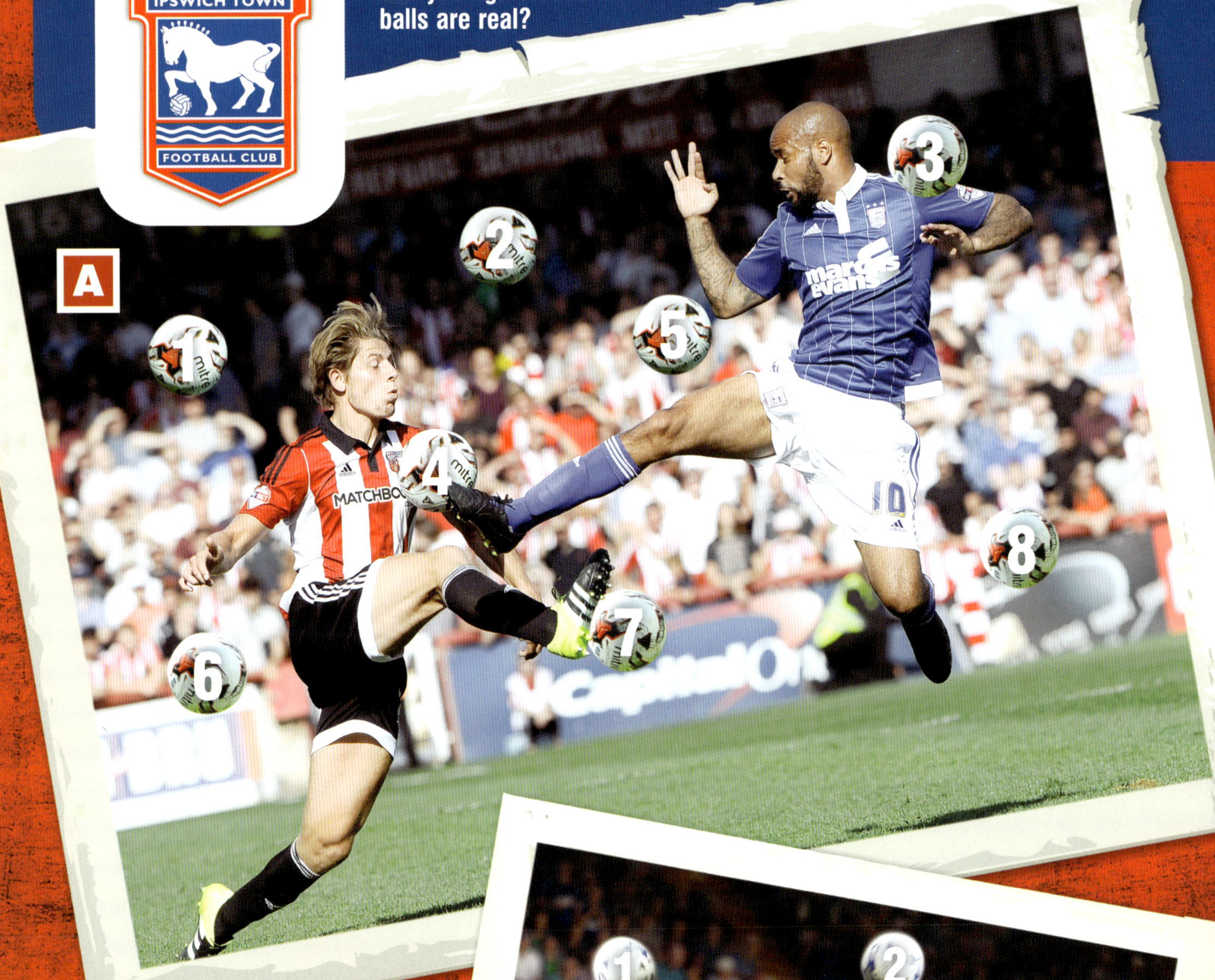

ANSWERS ON PAGE 62

RYAN
FRASER
14

BRETT PITMAN

FAVOURITES

- **Pizza?** Cheese & tomato
- **Film?** The Business
- **Actress?** Rachel McAdams
- **Song?** I listen to a wide mix
- **Sweets?** Haribo strawberries
- **Game?** I don't play games
- **Actor?** Denzel Washington
- **Animal?** Dog
- **Place?** Dubai
- **Colour?** Navy blue

What has been the best moment of your career?
Getting promoted three times with Bournemouth

Have you got any pre-match superstitions?
Yes, loads... but I'm not saying what they are!

What's your career advice for young talent out there?
Always work hard

What would your theme tune be? Batman

What is the funniest thing that has happened to you recently?
Spending time with Ryan Fraser is always a laugh!

Name three people, alive or dead, who you'd invite to your fantasy dinner party?
My fiancé, Pele and David Beckham

What's the most interesting thing we don't know about you?
I'm from the Channel Islands (Jersey)

LUKE CHAMBERS

FAVOURITES

- **Pizza?** Ham & Mushroom
- **Film?** The Matrix
- **Actor?** Denzel Washington
- **Actress?** Rachel McAdams
- **Animal?** Dog
- **Place?** Paris
- **Sweets?** White mice
- **Colour?** Blue
- **Song?** Baha Men, Who let the dogs out?
- **Game?** Lego, I'm a master builder!

Who is the toughest player you've played against? Ronaldo

What has been the best moment of your career?
Winning promotion with Forest

What's your career advice for young talent out there?
Be a good person, not just a good player

What is the funniest thing that has happened to you recently?
I spoke to Ryan Fraser!

If you were on an island and could only bring three things, what would you bring? Bread, butter and salt

Name three people, alive or dead, who you'd invite to your fantasy dinner party?
Denzel Washington, David Beckham and the wife

What's the most interesting thing we don't know about you?
I'm without doubt the best table tennis player at Ipswich!

LUKE HYAM

FAVOURITES

Pizza? Ham & pineapple	**Game?** Call of Duty
Film? Superbad	**Actor?** Tom Hardy
Actress? Rachel McAdams	**Animal?** Dog
Song? Mario, Let me love you	**Place?** Miami
Sweets? Fizzy strawberries	**Colour?** Black

What has been the best moment of your career?
Making my senior debut

Who do you most admire in football? Steven Gerrard

What's your career advice for young talent out there?
Work hard

What is your most annoying habit? Moodiness

If you were on an island and could only bring three things, what would you bring?
Phone, family and friends

Name three people, alive or dead, who you'd invite to your fantasy dinner party?
Anthony Joshua, David Beckham and Selena Gomez

What's the most interesting thing we don't know about you?
I'm good at everything I do!

JONATHAN DOUGLAS

FAVOURITES

Pizza? Ham & Mushroom	**Game?** Call of Duty
Film? In the name of the father	**Actor?** Daniel Day-Lewis
Actress? Rachel McAdams	**Animal?** Horse
Song? U2, One	**Place?** New York
Sweets? Chocolate raisins	**Colour?** Green

Who is the toughest player you've played against?
Robert Pires

Who do you most admire in football? Roy Keane

What's your career advice for young talent out there?
Work hard and enjoy it

What is your most annoying habit?
Moodiness - especially after a loss!

What is the funniest thing that has happened to you recently?
Meeting Luke Chambers

If you were on an island and could only bring three things, what would you bring?
My daughter, endless supply of sweets for her and an apple TV box so we can watch programmes

What's the most interesting thing we don't know about you?
I own three racehorses

IPSWICH TOWN
FOOTBALL CLUB
08
COLE
SKUSE

CULT heroes

Born: 10th November 1976, (Vucitrn, Yugoslavia)
Height: 6' 2"
Position: Striker

SHEFKI KUQI

Shefki Kuqi was a Finnish striker who joined Town from Sheffield Wednesday, initially on loan in 2003. From 2003 - 2005 Shefki made 90 appearances, scoring 34 goals. Kuqi joined on a permanent deal in November 2003, despite late interest from local rivals Norwich City. Shefki scored 20 goals in the 2004/05 season, finishing the joint top-goalscorer with Darren Bent. The Finn also picked up the Player of the Year award in 2005. Shefki returned for a brief loan spell at Portman Road in 2008, on loan from Crystal Palace.

Kuqi became a crowd favourite at Portman Road, not only for his goalscoring and tough, battling style of play, but also for his spectacular, unique, goal celebration. The 'Flying Finn', as he was dubbed by the media, would perform what was known as a Swan Dive.

Kuqi would jump with both arms out, almost attempting to glide through the air, before crashing to the ground. Ask any Blues' fan nowadays what they remember about Shefki and it's sure to be this outrageous celebration!

Whilst with Town, Shefki regularly represented his Finnish homeland internationally. Since retiring from the professional playing game Kuqi has turned to football management, managing FC Honka and more recently, PK-35 Vantaa.

TRAIN TO WIN

Footballers are getting fitter and fitter. Just as athletics records are broken, as runners get faster and faster, in football each generation of players are faster, fitter and stronger than before.

Clubs have more and more support staff, to provide everything a player will need to help him become the supreme athlete. These days, teams have fitness & conditioning coaches and nutritionists, who make sure every player is in the best physical shape he can be.

In pre-season, clubs carry out all kinds of tests on their players to monitor their progress and ensure each individual reaches and maintains peak fitness. A lot of work is done in the gym with weights, designed to make sure players have the strength not to be easily knocked off the ball and that they also possess the stamina to get through 90 minutes and not fade in the game's latter stages.

Of course, while fitness is essential, ultimately it is their ability that matters. Footballers like to train with the ball and work hard on their skills.

A lot of drills are undertaken to develop and maintain each player's ability on the ball. Coaching staff also work on team play, formations and developing understandings on the pitch.

A large proportion of goals come from set-pieces, so teams work on not just taking them, but defending free-kicks, corners and throw ins. Every team has a specialist dead-ball expert who they rely on for these important moments in games. Some teams prefer to do man-for-man marking and some use the zonal approach. In man-for-man marking, every player has a responsibility to mark a particular opponent, while zonal marking means, every player has an area of the pitch that they have to defend.

Whichever system is used, it is important that players work hard in training, so that they are a fully fit and well organised unit, and can perform together, successfully as a team.

A lot of work goes on behind the scenes at Ipswich Town.

Here's a look at the Blues' backroom staff.

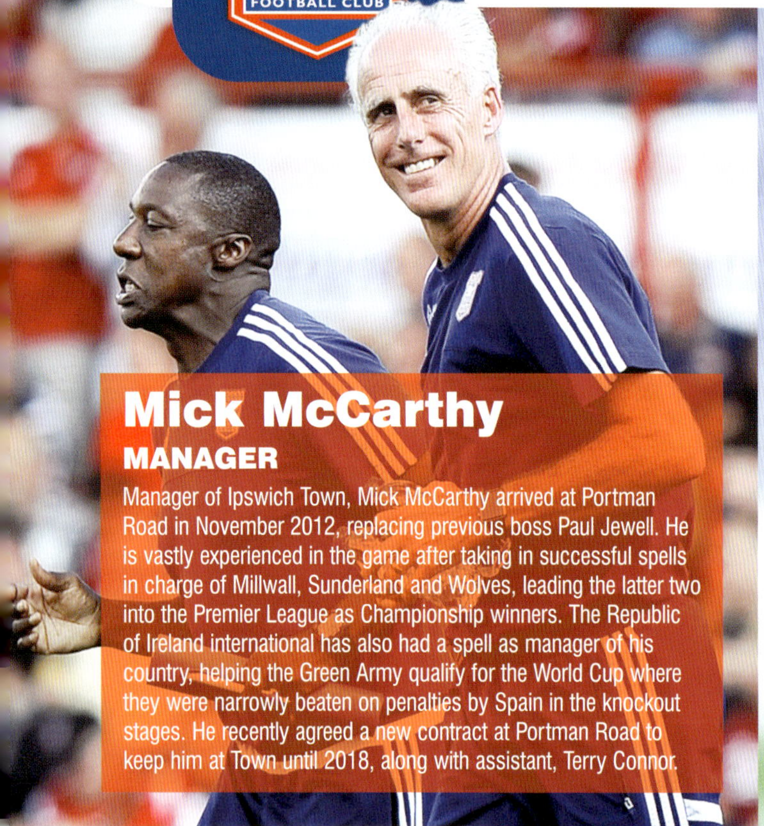

Mick McCarthy

MANAGER

Manager of Ipswich Town, Mick McCarthy arrived at Portman Road in November 2012, replacing previous boss Paul Jewell. He is vastly experienced in the game after taking in successful spells in charge of Millwall, Sunderland and Wolves, leading the latter two into the Premier League as Championship winners. The Republic of Ireland international has also had a spell as manager of his country, helping the Green Army qualify for the World Cup where they were narrowly beaten on penalties by Spain in the knockout stages. He recently agreed a new contract at Portman Road to keep him at Town until 2018, along with assistant, Terry Connor.

Terry Connor

ASSISTANT MANAGER

Right-hand man to Mick McCarthy, Terry Connor arrived at the Club on the same day as the manager. He had worked alongside the current Town boss at Wolves, before then taking over at Molinuex as manager following Mick's departure until the end of the season. He was unable to prevent the Midlanders from dropping out of the Premier League but remained on the coaching staff at Wolves, before departing shortly after the following season began. He linked up with Mick again at Portman Road in November 2012 and has established himself as a popular figure with both the players, staff and fans-alike.

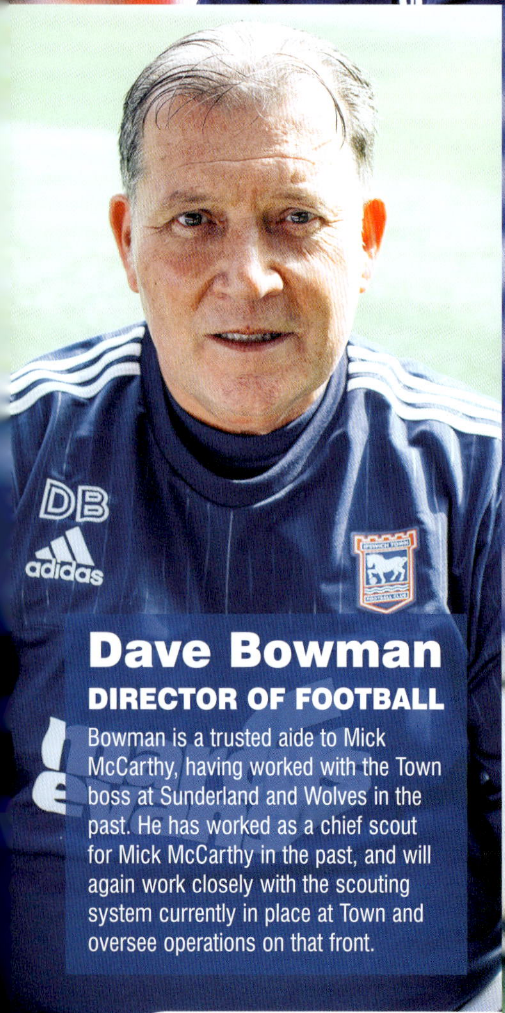

Dave Bowman

DIRECTOR OF FOOTBALL

Bowman is a trusted aide to Mick McCarthy, having worked with the Town boss at Sunderland and Wolves in the past. He has worked as a chief scout for Mick McCarthy in the past, and will again work closely with the scouting system currently in place at Town and oversee operations on that front.

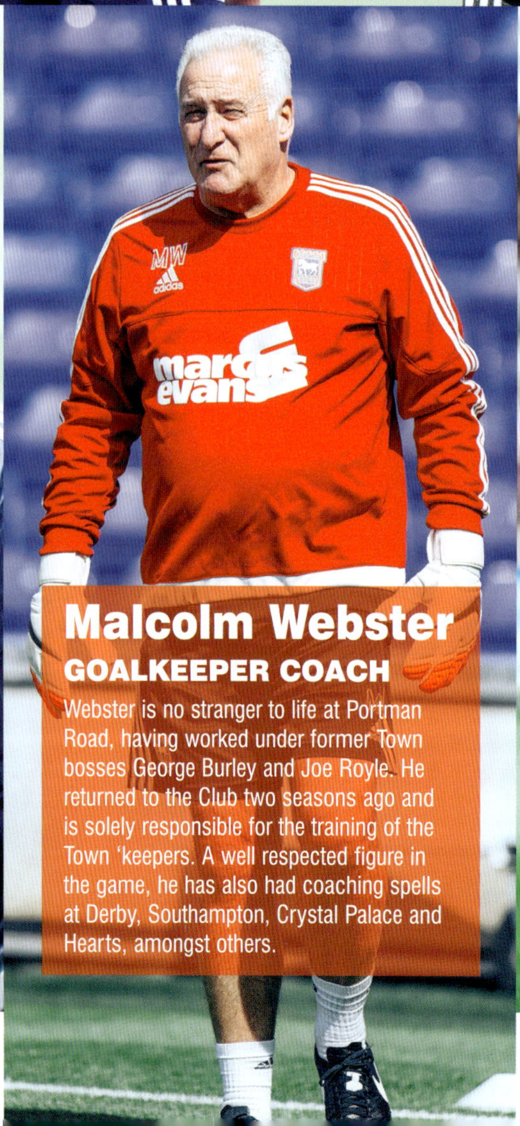

Malcolm Webster

GOALKEEPER COACH

Webster is no stranger to life at Portman Road, having worked under former Town bosses George Burley and Joe Royle. He returned to the Club two seasons ago and is solely responsible for the training of the Town 'keepers. A well respected figure in the game, he has also had coaching spells at Derby, Southampton, Crystal Palace and Hearts, amongst others.

Andy Liddell

FITNESS COACH

Former midfielder for Barnsley (who he helped win promotion to the Premier League), Wigan, Sheffield United, Oldham and Rotherham, before hanging up his boots in 2010. Lidds previously played under Paul Jewell at Wigan and the former Town boss wasted little time in recruiting him as Blues' fitness coach. He is responsible for ensuring that the Town squad maintain their peak fitness levels throughout the season and can be seen putting the players through their paces in the warm-up before matches.

Bryan Klug
ACADEMY DIRECTOR

Klug returned to Portman Road prior to the start of the 2012/13 season to head up the Town Academy. He is a well respected figure around the Club having previously helped the Town youngsters win the FA Youth Cup in 2005, and later going on to assist former boss Jim Magilton.

Mark Kennedy
U21S MANAGER

A former Town player, Kennedy joined the coaching staff at the end of the 2011/12 season, upon his retirement as a player. He now oversees the Town U21 Development Squad.

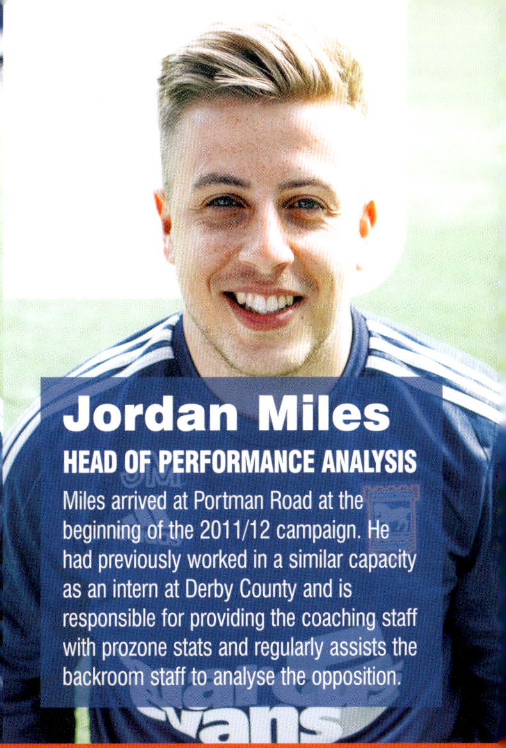

Jordan Miles
HEAD OF PERFORMANCE ANALYSIS

Miles arrived at Portman Road at the beginning of the 2011/12 campaign. He had previously worked in a similar capacity as an intern at Derby County and is responsible for providing the coaching staff with prozone stats and regularly assists the backroom staff to analyse the opposition.

THE TEAM BEHIND THE TEAM

Alex Chapman
ASSISTANT HEAD PHYSIO

Working alongside Town's Head Physio Matt Byard, Chapman is first on the scene to treat the players when they pick up any form of injury. He will be working with the first-team squad this season, after joining the backroom staff from a similar position in the Town Academy.

James Pullen
KITMAN

A former Town goalkeeper, Pullen is now working as part of the backroom staff at Portman Road as kitman. He manages all of the equipment and kit for the Blues on matchdays. Has the nickname 'Horse' around the Club after running the London marathon dressed as ITFC mascot, Crazee!

Matt Byard
HEAD PHYSIO

Byard is Town's Head Physio and is always first on the scene whenever a Blues player goes down with an injury. He has held the role for some time now and is an integral part of Mick McCarthy's backroom staff.

ON THE ROAD

Can you work out which Championship teams these away shirts belong to?

1

2

3

4

5

6

7

8

9
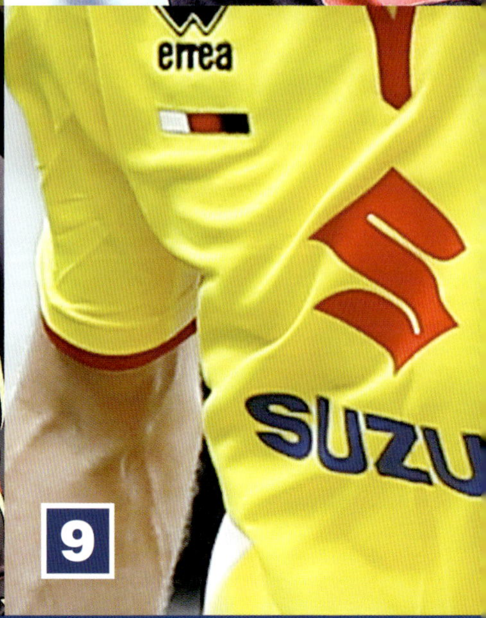

ANSWERS ON PAGE 62

LUKE
CHAMBERS
04

STAND OUT

There are five British actors hidden in the crowd... can you find them all?

FROM THE CROWD...

ANSWERS ON PAGE 62

IPSWICH TOWN
FOOTBALL CLUB
16 GILES COKE
adidas
marcus evans
mitre

NAME THAT TEAM...

Here are the nicknames of every Championship Club, can you work out who the team is and then find them in the grid?

1. Robins ______
2. Rovers ______
3. Royals ______
4. Boro ______
5. Cottagers ______
6. Clarets ______
7. Bluebirds ______
8. Blues ______
9. Seagulls ______
10. Terriers ______
11. Bees ______
12. Tigers ______
13. Whites ______
14. Hoops ______
15. The Dons ______
16. Wolves ______
17. Millers ______
18. Owls ______
19. Forest ______
20. Trotters ______
21. Lilywhites ______
22. Tractor Boys ______
23. Addicks ______
24. Rams ______

P	H	U	D	D	E	R	S	F	I	E	L	D	T	O	W	N	O	C	N	C	Q
A	R	I	S	E	P	M	M	E	G	T	H	U	H	A	O	A	B	I	B	H	U
U	A	E	L	Y	T	I	C	L	O	T	S	I	R	B	L	W	H	H	E	A	E
L	I	P	S	W	I	C	H	T	O	W	N	S	K	M	V	S	G	U	C	R	E
A	T	M	G	T	K	B	A	F	R	B	F	N	B	H	E	T	U	L	Z	L	N
Q	S	Y	P	E	O	L	U	K	G	N	I	D	A	E	R	R	O	L	P	T	S
W	E	T	I	E	B	N	H	R	U	S	T	P	E	O	H	T	R	C	S	O	P
B	R	I	G	H	T	O	N	A	N	D	H	O	V	E	A	L	B	I	O	N	A
I	O	C	I	D	I	G	R	O	A	L	C	S	I	H	M	U	S	T	S	A	R
R	F	F	Y	V	J	A	D	Q	R	C	E	J	A	V	P	S	E	Y	Q	T	K
M	M	F	D	G	W	K	F	O	C	T	I	Y	T	S	T	K	L	T	U	H	R
I	A	I	O	F	M	S	E	G	U	O	H	B	K	A	O	I	D	I	W	L	A
N	H	D	D	E	T	I	N	U	S	D	E	E	L	S	N	R	D	G	H	E	N
G	G	R	A	N	K	E	M	D	V	A	U	E	N	D	W	O	I	E	W	T	G
H	N	A	N	F	C	A	N	Z	L	F	B	I	S	D	A	Y	M	R	S	I	E
A	I	C	T	J	H	D	R	O	F	T	N	E	R	B	N	D	Q	S	R	C	R
M	T	X	O	L	C	B	O	L	T	O	N	W	A	N	D	E	R	E	R	S	S
C	T	Y	U	Y	A	D	S	E	N	D	E	W	D	L	E	I	F	F	E	H	S
I	O	F	M	W	U	J	Y	T	N	U	O	C	Y	B	R	E	D	B	E	X	Y
T	N	P	B	L	A	C	K	B	U	R	N	R	O	V	E	R	S	P	G	I	A
Y	D	E	T	I	N	U	M	A	H	R	E	H	T	O	R	V	I	W	K	O	N
E	P	A	S	T	B	D	O	X	M	P	L	O	N	E	S	Y	C	S	W	B	H

ANSWERS ON PAGE 62

TOMMY SMITH

FAVOURITES

Pizza topping? Pepperoni
Film? Black Hawk Down
Actress? Eva Mendes
Place? Dubai
Colour? Blue
Game? Skipbo (NZ game)
Actor? Liam Neeson
Animal? Cat
Sweets? Haribo Starmix
Song? Ed Sheeran, Thinking out loud

Who is the toughest player you've played against?
Neymar

What has been the best moment of your career?
Playing at the World Cup for New Zealand

Who do you most admire in football?
Lionel Messi

Have you got any pre-match superstitions?
I always have beans on toast as a pre-match meal!

What's your career advice for young talent out there?
Attitude trumps talent

What is your most annoying habit?
Biting my nails

What would your theme tune be?
My Way, Frank Sinatra

What is the funniest thing that has happened to you recently?
I did a 'Bungee Run'

If you were on an island and could only bring three things, what would you bring?
My girlfriend, a boat and a machete

Name three people, alive or dead, who you'd invite to your fantasy dinner party?
Mike Tyson, Leonardo DiCaprio and Emmanuelle Chriqui

What's the most interesting thing we don't know about you? I'm currently studying for a degree in Sports Science

DARYL MURPHY

FAVOURITES

Pizza topping? Chicken
Film? Dumb & Dumber
Actress? Jessica Alba
Song? Bastille, Pompeii
Sweets? Haribo
Game? Call of Duty
Actor? Tom Hardy
Animal? Dog
Place? Dubai
Colour? Blue

What has been the best moment of your career?
Playing for my country (Ireland)

Who do you most admire in football?
David Beckham

What's your career advice for young talent out there?
Enjoy it and work as hard as you possibly can

What would your theme tune be? Rocky

What is the funniest thing that has happened to you recently? Ryan Fraser asking if a tattoo of a cross would fit on his arm - priceless!

Name three people, alive or dead, who you'd invite to your fantasy dinner party?
The wife, Jessica Alba and Rita Ora

What's the most interesting thing we don't know about you?
I'm a decent singer

FREDDIE SEARS

FAVOURITES

Pizza topping? Chicken
Film? The Hangover
Actress? Rachel McAdams
Song? Calvin Harris, Feel so close
Sweets? I prefer chocolate!
Game? FIFA
Actor? Tom Hardy
Animal? Dog
Place? Florida
Colour? Black

Who is the toughest player you've played against?
Rio Ferdinand

What has been the best moment of your career?
Scoring on my Premier League debut for West Ham

Have you got any pre-match superstitions?
I always put my right boot on first

What is your most annoying habit? Biting my nails

If you were on an island and could only bring three things, what would you bring?
My phone, laptop and a charger

Name three people, alive or dead, who you'd invite to your fantasy dinner party?
Beckham, Messi and Ronaldo

What's the most interesting thing we don't know about you?
I've met the Queen before

How much do you know about Ipswich Town's last year?

TEST YOURSELF ON 2015 IPSWICH TOWN

01

Blues signed a Danish international defender from Esbjerg this season. Who is he?

02

Ipswich Town's highest home attendance last season was 29,166 but who were they playing?

03

Against whom was the Tractor Boys' first League win of the calendar year?

04

Name the midfielder who joined Ipswich this summer after being released by Sheffield Wednesday.

05

Cole Skuse received the Goal of the Season award this year, but who were Blues playing when he made his winning strike?

06

For how many more years did Daryl Murphy extend his contract in July 2015?

07

Who are the Blues playing in their last game of 2015?

Take our test and find out!

08

Which Irish team did the Blues beat 6-0 in a pre-season friendly in July 2015?

09

Which young Arsenal talent joined Ipswich on a season-long loan for the 2015/16 season?

10

Which Ipswich Town player has gone out on loan to Portsmouth this season?

11

Who were the Blues joint top appearance makers last season and how many total appearances did they each make?

12

Ipswich played FC Utrecht in a pre-season friendly match this July. Which country are they from?

13

Daryl Murphy finished the 2014/15 season as Championship top scorer.

How many goals did he score?

14

Larsen Touré is now a permanent member of the ITFC squad since he switched from Arles-Avignon on a free transfer this summer.

Which international team has he represented?

15

Who scored the first goal for the Tractor Boys this season?

ANSWERS ON PAGE 62

MARTIJN REUSER

Martijn Reuser began his professional career at Dutch side Ajax. The skilful, goalscoring midfielder played for Ajax before moving to Vitesse. Whilst at Vitesse, Martijn made his one and only appearance for the Dutch national team in a friendly match against Ghana.

Reuser moved to Town after being scouted by Romeo Zondervan for George Burley's men. On his debut, Martijn scored the winner, coming on as a substitute against Fulham. From that day, Town fans took the Dutchman to their hearts.

Reuser was to score another goal in an epic Play-Off Semi-Final against Bolton, setting up the 1999/2000 season Play-Off Final at Wembley against Barnsley. Having reached the Play-Offs in the previous three seasons, but never reaching Wembley, Town were desperate to put a stop to this run of heartache. A highly controversial Semi-Final second leg was sealed with Reuser's goal, 5-3 on the night and 7-5 on aggregate, with Bolton giving away three penalties and having two men sent off!

The Final was a close fought game. Barnsley were competing in their first Play-Off final. Taking the lead through a Richard Wright own goal after only six minutes, Barnsley started to dream. However Town hit back with goals through Tony Mowbray, Richard Naylor and Marcus Stewart. Barnsley were awarded a penalty in the 78th minute which Craig Hignett scored to make the score 3-2 to Town. With the match finely balanced and Barnsley pushing for an equaliser, Reuser, an 83rd minute substitute, broke a high Barnsley line, after being put through by Naylor, to smash home emphatically from the edge of the box after a run from just inside the Barnsley half.

The 'Flying Dutchman' had sealed Town's promotion to the Premier League in stoppage time.

Born: 1st February 1975 (Amsterdam, Netherlands)
Height: 5' 9"
Position: Midfielder

29 JOSH EMMANUEL

DANGER MEN

Every team have players who can hurt you.

Take a look at the Championship's Danger Men

BLACKBURN ROVERS

JORDAN RHODES

Goal machine Jordan grew up with inside knowledge about how to beat goalkeepers. His dad, Andy was a former goalkeeper and was goalkeeping coach at Ipswich Town, where Jordan developed as a youngster. Following a trio of loans, he came to life at Huddersfield with 73 goals in 124 games and since becoming Blackburn's record signing has more than matched that tally.

BRENTFORD

JOTA

The Spanish midfielder won Brentford's 'Outstanding Moment of the Season' award, for his winner in the derby with Fulham and was nominated for the Bees' 2014 Mitre Goal of the Year award for his strike against Cardiff City. Technically gifted, Jota played for Real Madrid's 'B' team three years ago.

BIRMINGHAM CITY

DEMARAI GRAY

The teenager, who scored Blues' Goal of the Season against Wolves, when he ran from his own half, also bagged a hat-trick against Reading. Birmingham-born winger Demarai has the kind of pace and dribbling ability that scares defenders and has already been capped at U20 level by England.

BOLTON WANDERERS

EMILE HESKEY

Bolton rank former England striker Emile Heskey within their squad, adding both power and experience to their frontline. The forward, who Premier League giants Liverpool once splashed out £8m on for his services, joined the Trotters on a short-term deal last season and made an immediate impact, as he scored on his debut. Although now edging well into his twilight years, the striker is still a threat at Championship level and someone who can cause problems in the final third.

BRIGHTON & HOVE ALBION

KAZENGA LUALUA

The scorer of Albion's first goal of the season, Kazenga LuaLua is an exciting player, who on his day can cause havoc in opposing defences with his power and trickery. He also struck a cracker against Ipswich Town in an early-season encounter. Having come through the ranks at Newcastle United, Kazenga has now played over 100 games for the Seagulls.

BRISTOL CITY

JONATHAN KODJIA

Last season's French Ligue 2 Player of the Year arrived at Ashton Gate in the summer. The pacey Ivorian striker scored 15 goals in 29 games last season, firing Angers to promotion to the top flight in France. Kodjia wasted no time in showing he had not left his goal touch across the channel, marking his home debut with a goal against Brentford and bagging another against Burnley before the end of August.

CARDIFF CITY

KENWYNE JONES

The spectacular sight of a Kenwyne Jones celebration somersault is something all Bluebirds fans love to see. The tall Trinidadian was once described as the most dangerous player in the game in the air by John Terry and certainly, on his day, no one can keep up with Kenwyne.

DERBY COUNTY

TOM INCE

Eleven goals in 18 games on loan last season persuaded the Rams to pay Hull City a reported £4.75m for the son of former England midfielder Paul. Tom is fast, two-footed, tricky and draws people to the ball, before releasing it at just the right moment. He could be the man to take Derby County to the top.

BURNLEY

ANDRE GRAY

Burnley smashed their transfer record to buy Andre Gray from Brentford, for a reported £9m fee. After bagging 18 goals for the Bees last season, Gray scored in the first two matches of this season, including one against newly promoted Bristol City, who wanted to sign him, but Burnley stepped in to snap him up and will look to the former Luton Town man to fire them straight back into the top flight.

CHARLTON ATHLETIC

SIMON MAKIENOK

You can not miss Makienok, standing 6'7" with his blond ponytail! His has a real physical presence. Not only do his knock-downs put the ball in the danger-area for the Addicks attackers, but he is more than useful in his own box too, defending set-pieces.The Dane is a vital player for the men from the Valley.

FULHAM

ROSS McCORMACK

Scotland international McCormack, cost the Whites £11m in July 2014, an astonishing fee for a newly-relegated club. He proved his worth by netting 19 goals in 50 appearances. An impressive stat, given that he does not always play as an out-and-out striker. His all-round play often means that he is employed in a deeper role, where he is more involved in the game. If Fulham are to do well, McCormack will be a main man.

HUDDERSFIELD TOWN

NAHKI WELLS

Bermuda international Nahki Wells, became the Terriers record signing when he moved from Bradford City. He smashed 25 goals for City in 2012/13, which included strikes in the Play-Off final and the Capital One Cup semi-final against Villa. Nahki notched 14 goals last season, in his first full campaign with Huddersfield and with his pace and persistence, he will always spell danger for the opposition.

LEEDS UNITED

MIRCO ANTENUCCI

The veteran Italian striker has represented nine clubs in his own country, including Torino, with whom he won promotion to Serie 'A' in 2011/12. Muscular and mobile, Mirco hit double figures for Leeds last season and scored a stunner against Burnley to start the current campaign with a bang.

MK DONS

DIEGO POYET

The 20-year-old son of Gus Poyet, England U20 international midfielder Diego made five Europa League appearances for West Ham this season, before joining MK Dons. His passing ability and footballing philosophy fits snugly into the Dons renowned possession game. Poyet was Charlton's Young Player of the Year, the season before last, despite not debuting until January of that campaign.

HULL CITY

MOSES ODUBAJO

Looking to bounce straight back to the top flight, the Tigers invested a reported £3.5m to capture England U20 Moses Odubajo from Brentford. He missed just one game last season as the Bees just missed out on promotion, losing in the Play-Off semi final. A right-winger or right-back, Moses spent four years with Leyton Orient winning the O's Goal of the Season in 2011/12 and voted their Young Player of the Year, the following season.

MIDDLESBROUGH

STEWART DOWNING

Boro splashed the cash, paying a reported £7m to bring Stewart Downing back to his first club, after a stellar season for West Ham. Starting out as a sizzling winger, Downing has developed into a player whose vision lets him create chances from a more central position, as well as always posing a threat himself.

NOTTINGHAM FOREST

BRITT ASSOMBALONGA

Britt Assombalonga will not be fit until the second half of the season, but he could be the man to fire Forest to promotion, if they can keep themselves in the running until then. Britt had scored 15 times before his injury in February, a tally that gives him over 50 in the last three years.

PRESTON NORTH END

DANIEL JOHNSON

Daniel's eight goals in the second half of last season, after joining in January, helped North End to promotion. Having earlier scored three times on loan to Oldham, Jamaican-born Johnson, was in double figures for the season and after getting off to a good start with the first home goal at Deepdale this season, will hope to reach that target again.

READING

OLA JOHN

John signed for the Royals on a season -long loan in the summer from Benfica. He is a very talented forward with power, pace, the ability to beat his man, deliver quality balls into the box and also has an eye for goal himself. With all these attributes, Ola should help ensure Reading are a potent offensive force this campaign.

SHEFFIELD WEDNESDAY

MARCO MATIAS

Matias' early-season goal at Leeds marked him out as a special player. The way he lobbed the ball over Liam Cooper before applying the most spectacular finish, was pure quality. Last season he scored 17 goals in 33 games in the Portuguese top flight for CD Nacional, while home fans saw his first goal at Hillsborough come against Middlesbrough in August.

QUEENS PARK RANGERS

CHARLIE AUSTIN

Barclays Premier League Player of the Month for December 2014, Charlie was called up by England, although he still awaits his first cap. QPR fans were relieved he did not move on in the transfer window, as many clubs were understandably keen on signing a player who has scored well over 100 goals for QPR, Burnley and Swindon after making his name in non-league football.

ROTHERHAM UNITED

JORDAN BOWERY

Bowery impressed so much as a youngster at Chesterfield, that Aston Villa spent £500,000 on him when he was only 21. Jordan is an impact player, with 28 of his 36 appearances last term coming off the bench, but a clue to his quality was that two of his five goals came against teams subsequently promoted to the Barclays Premier League.

WOLVERHAMPTON WANDERERS

BENIK AFOBE

Goals, goals, goals are what Afobe is all about. He struck three times in the first four games of this season after scoring 32 last term, 13 of them after his move to Molineux from MK Dons. The 22-year -old came through the ranks at Arsenal and the England U21 international was reportedly, the subject of a £12m bid from Norwich City in August.

IPSWICH TOWN
FOOTBALL CLUB
DAVID
McGOLDRICK
10

Put your creative talents to the test...

DESIGN A NEW KIT

TEST YOURSELF ON 2015 THE CHAMPIONSHIP

How much do you know about the teams in the Sky Bet Championship?

01
BIRMINGHAM CITY
What was Blues' highest home attendance last season?

02
BLACKBURN ROVERS
Who was Blackburn's top League goal scorer of the 2014/15 season?

03

BOLTON WANDERERS
Who was Bolton's first signing this summer?

04
BRENTFORD
The Bees finished fifth last season and made it to the Play-Offs. But who were they defeated by in the semi-finals?

05
BRIGHTON & HOVE ALBION
The Seagulls are the most southern team in the Championship. True or false?

06
BRISTOL CITY
Bristol City were promoted as Champions this season, how many points did they top the League One table with?

07
BURNLEY
Who scored the Clarets' first goal of the 2015/16 season?

08

CARDIFF CITY
Cardiff is the only Welsh team in the Championship. True or false?

09

CHARLTON ATHLETIC
Which shot stopper is wearing the No.1 jersey for the Addicks this season?

10

DERBY COUNTY
Derby got a new manager this season to replace Steve McClaren. Who is he?

11
FULHAM
Name the Fulham player who scored two hat-tricks last season!

12
HUDDERSFIELD TOWN
Who made the most appearances in total for the Terriers' last season?

Take our test and find out!

13

HULL CITY

Who was Hull City's £1.3m summer signing from Chesterfield this season?

14

IPSWICH TOWN

Who was the the Tractor Boys' first summer 2015/16 signing from Cardiff City?

15

LEEDS UNITED

Uwe Rosler is Leeds' new manager this season. Who did he replace?

16

MIDDLESBROUGH

Boro had the highest attendance of 33,381 in the Championship last term. Who were they playing?

17

MK DONS

Who is captaining MK Dons this season?

18

NOTTINGHAM FOREST

A Forest player received the Player of the Month award in February 2015. **Who was it?**

19

PRESTON NORTH END

What colour is the Lilywhites' away kit this season?

20

QUEENS PARK RANGERS

Who was first to sign for the Hoops' this summer on a free transfer from Bristol City?

21

READING

Who was Reading's first League win of the 2015/16 season against?

22

ROTHERHAM UNITED

Which hot shot is wearing the No.9 jersey for the Millers this season?

23

SHEFFIELD WEDNESDAY

Who will the Owls play in their last game of 2015?

24

WOLVERHAMPTON WANDERERS

Wolves have a new sponsor this season. Who is it?

ANSWERS ON PAGE 62

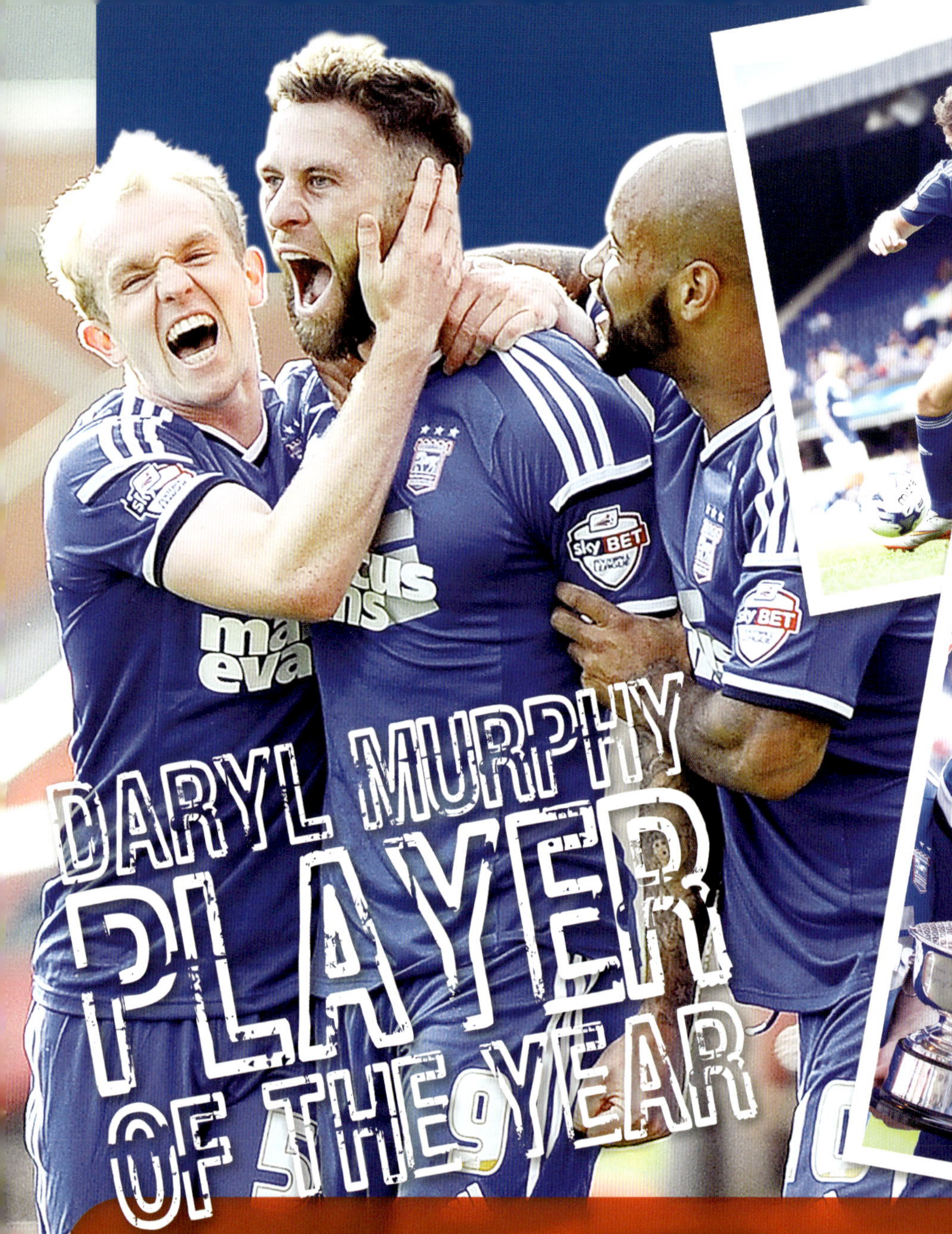

DARYL MURPHY PLAYER OF THE YEAR

Daryl Murphy picked up numerous awards for his efforts in the 2014/15 season. The Irish striker bagged the Town Supporters' Player of the Year, Junior Blues' Player of the Year and also the Players' Player of the Year accolades. Murphy also secured a place in the PFA Championship Team of the Year and was shortlisted, in the top three, for SkyBet Championship Player of the Year, after bagging the December monthly award.

Daryl is in his fourth spell at Portman Road having spent three previous terms with Town on loan from Sunderland and Celtic respectively. Having signed permanently on 7th June 2013, Murphy has quickly established himself as one of the leading marksmen in the Championship, netting 40 goals over the course of the 2013/14 and 2014/15 seasons. It's easy to see why Daryl is a fans' favourite at Portman Road!

Town's Player of the Year had a phenomenal 2014/15 season, finishing as the Championship's top scorer with 27 goals to his name, leading to appearances in the Republic of Ireland national team and securing a two-year contract extension with Ipswich Town FC. His aerial prowess and natural instinct to shoot-on-sight led to Daryl being the target of much transfer speculation, however he put pen to paper on an extended contract stating,

"I have always said I'm happy and settled here and that has never changed. I have never thought about moving and now, having signed a new contract, I can put all that speculation talk to bed and look forward to the new season."

Murphy has always been a powerful centre-forward, offering great hold-up play, linking up with other strikers, however more recently he has added more goals to his game... lots more goals! Alongside David McGoldrick, Freddie Sears and the recently acquired Brett Pitman, they form a formidable front line for Town heading into the 2015/16 season which will hopefully see many Championship defences struggling to contain them with Town pushing hard to go one better than the Play-Off spot finish of 2014/15.

Danny Haynes is a more recent cult hero that the rest. In 2005 Haynes was part of the Ipswich Town youth team who won the FA Youth Cup, beating Southampton over two legs to lift the coveted silverware.

Born: 19th January 1988 (Peckham, England)
Height: 6' 0"
Position: Striker

DANNY HAYNES

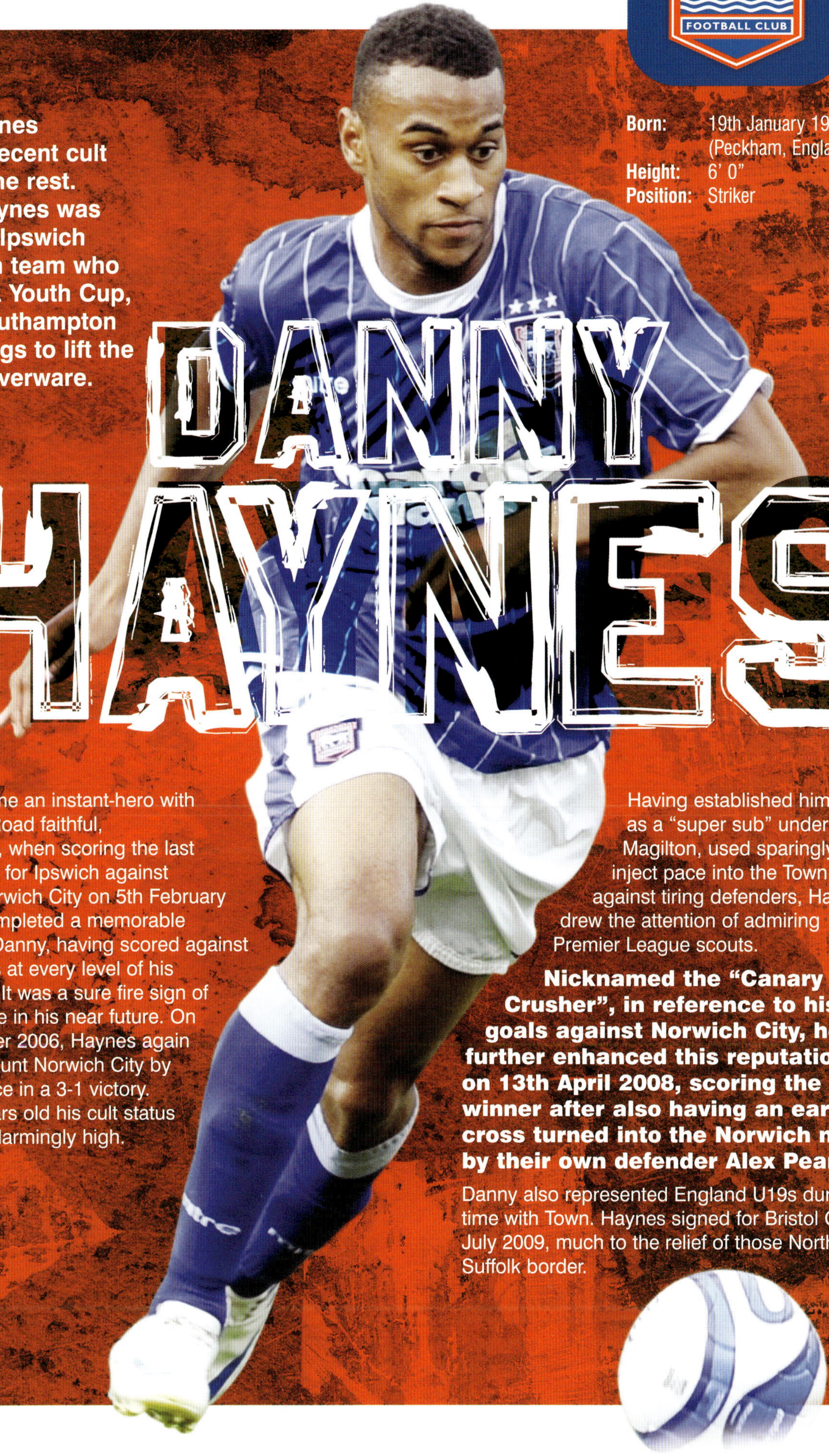

Haynes became an instant-hero with the Portman Road faithful, unsurprisingly, when scoring the last minute winner for Ipswich against arch-rivals Norwich City on 5th February 2006. This completed a memorable accolade for Danny, having scored against the local rivals at every level of his development. It was a sure fire sign of things to come in his near future. On 19th November 2006, Haynes again returned to haunt Norwich City by scoring a brace in a 3-1 victory. At only 18 years old his cult status was already alarmingly high.

Having established himself as a "super sub" under Jim Magilton, used sparingly to inject pace into the Town attack against tiring defenders, Haynes drew the attention of admiring Premier League scouts.

Nicknamed the "Canary Crusher", in reference to his goals against Norwich City, he further enhanced this reputation on 13th April 2008, scoring the winner after also having an earlier cross turned into the Norwich net by their own defender Alex Pearce!

Danny also represented England U19s during his time with Town. Haynes signed for Bristol City in July 2009, much to the relief of those North of the Suffolk border.

SPOT THE DIFFERENCE

Can you find the eight differences between these two celebration shots?!

ANSWERS ON PAGE 62

09
DARYL
MURPHY
IPSWICH TOWN
FOOTBALL CLUB
marcus evans

Can you identify these Blues stars?

ANSWERS ON PAGE 62

CULT heroes

JOHN Wark

BORN: 4th August 1957 (Glasgow, Scotland)
HEIGHT: 5' 11"
POSITION: Attacking Midfielder

John Wark is an Ipswich Town FC legend. He won a record four Player of the Year awards before becoming one of four inaugural members of the Ipswich Town Football Club Hall of Fame. Wark played for Ipswich Town in three long spells covering 17 years (1975-84, 1988-90 and 1991-97). A versatile player John played most of his games for Town in midfield, however he also covered as a centre-back and striker throughout his time in Suffolk.

Wark made his debut for Town on 27th March 1975 for Bobby Robson's men in an FA Cup 6th Round, 3rd replay tie against Leeds United at Filbert Street, Leicester. Playing regularly for the youth team and reserves, Wark established himself as a first team regular in the 1976/77 season, playing 30 games in midfield, scoring 10 goals. Over the next five years John was a regular in the Town team that won the FA Cup, UEFA Cup and came within one game of winning the League Championship on two occasions, finishing as runners-up to Liverpool and Aston Villa.

Winning the UEFA Cup in 1981 was John's greatest ever achievement within the professional game. He scored an amazing 36 goals in the 1980/81 season. This fantastic record helped John pick up the European Young Player of the Year award and the PFA's Player of the Year award.

Within his three spells at Ipswich Town, John amassed 190 goals in almost 700 appearances, and sits second in Town's all time goalscorer and all time appearances records.

John played a character called Arthur Hayes in the 1981 file 'Escape to Victory' alongside Sylvester Stallone and Michael Caine. However his only line was dubbed due to his broad Glaswegian accent! Wark also published an autobiography, titled Wark On, in 2009.

It was a cold Tuesday night, under the floodlights, at Portman Road that Cole Skuse found himself running on to a poor clearance from a Cardiff City centre-back. The rest as they so often say..... is history!

Skuse was 30 yards from goal and hit a crisp first time half-volley which flew into the back of the net in front of the Sir Alf Ramsey Stand, giving the Cardiff keeper no chance. Nobody in the stadium was more surprised than Cole himself. It brought to an end a three-year goal drought in stunning style. It was only the 10th goal of his career and first in 82 appearances in the blue and white of Ipswich Town.

Town went on to win the match 3-1 on the night with goals from Freddie Sears and Daryl Murphy either side of the Skuse wonderstrike. The win kept the Blues in contention for a Play-Off place with only a handful of games remaining in the season. It may be Cole's only goal for Town so far but it is one of the best that has been seen at Portman Road for many years.

The goal eased to victory at the end of season awards ceremony allowing Skuse to pick up the Goal of the Season award, alongside the John Kerridge Memorial Trophy - the winner selected by manager Mick McCarthy. Cole was also nominated for the SkyBet Championship Player of the Month award for April 2015.

COLE SKUSE
GOAL
OF THE SEASON
IPSWICH 3 - 1 CARDIFF
TUESDAY 14 APRIL 2015

07 AINSLEY MAITLAND-NILES

PUZZLE IT OUT

CAREER WATCH

Work out the missing teams in David McGoldrick's career.

2004	Notts County
2004-2009	ANSWER
2009-2013	ANSWER
2013 - Present	Ipswich Town

Who are yer?

Three Blues players are mixed up in this picture!

DERBY DAY

Can you match each team to their rival?

1

2

3

4

HOMELANDS

Match the player to their home country

Mauritius	Jonathan Parr
Kevin Bru	Scotland
Poland	Daryl Murphy
Bartosz Bialkowski	New Zealand
Norway	Christophe Berra
Tommy Smith	Republic of Ireland

ANSWERS ON PAGE 62

We've set you a huge challenge for the new year!

Every month there are two new tasks to complete.

2016 CHALLENGE

JANUARY

- ☐ Do 25 keepy-uppies
- ☐ Come up with a new ITFC chant!

FEBRUARY

- ☐ Take a selfie at a Championship Stadium
- ☐ Learn a new trick - around the world!

MARCH

- ☐ Nutmeg someone!
- ☐ Get an autograph from a Blues player

APRIL

- ☐ Do 50 keepy-uppies
- ☐ Take a selfie with a Blues player

MAY

- ☐ Work on your fitness - run 1 mile!
- ☐ Lob the keeper

Have you got what it takes?!

JUNE

- Learn a new trick - catch the ball on your neck
- Set up a sponsored event with your mates and do your bit for charity!

JULY

- Learn a new trick - keepy-uppies with a tennis ball
- Work on your fitness - run 3 miles!

AUGUST

- Take a selfie with a Blues legend
- Do 75 keepy-uppies

SEPTEMBER

- Do 10 keepy-uppies on your head
- Try out for your school footie team

OCTOBER

- Shake Bluey's hand
- Take a selfie with Mick McCarthy

NOVEMBER

- Work on your fitness - run 5 miles!
- Score from the penalty spot by hitting the underside of the crossbar

DECEMBER

- Do 100 keepy-uppies
- Start a chant at the match

ANSWERS

PAGE 20 · WHAT BALL?

Picture A - Ball 4, Picture B - Ball 2

PAGE 30 · ON THE ROAD

1. Cardiff City, 2. Rotherham United, 3. Leeds United,
4. Brighton & Hove Albion, 5. Middlesbrough, 6. Derby County,
7. Burnley, 8. Birmingham City, 9. MK Dons

PAGE 32 · STAND OUT FROM THE CROWD

Emma Watson, Idris Elba, Andrew Lincoln,
Benedict Cumberbatch and Keira Knightley

PAGE 35 · NAME THAT TEAM...

1. Robins - Bristol City, 2. Rovers - Blackburn Rovers,
3. Royals - Reading, 4. Boro - Middlesbrough, 5. Cottagers - Fulham,
6. Clarets - Burnley, 7. Bluebirds - Cardiff City, 8. Blues - Birmingham City
9. Seagulls - Brighton and Hove Albion, 10. Terriers - Huddersfield Town,
11. Bees - Brentford, 12. Tigers - Hull City,
13. Whites - Leeds United, 14. Hoops - Queens Park Rangers
15. The Dons - MK Dons, 16. Wolves - Wolverhampton Wanderers
17. Millers - Rotherham United, 18. Owls - Sheffield Wednesday
19. Forest - Nottingham Forest, 20. Trotters - Bolton Wanderers
21. Lilywhites - Preston North End, 22. Tractor Boys - Ipswich Town
23. Addicks - Charlton Athletic, 24. Rams - Derby County

PAGE 38
TEST YOURSELF ON 2015, IPSWICH TOWN

1. Jonas Knudsen, 2. Norwich, 3. Millwall, 4. Giles Coke,
5. Cardiff City, 6. 2 years, 7. Brighton & Hove Albion, 8. Shelbourne
9. Ainsley Maitland-Niles, 10. Matt Clarke, 11. Luke Chambers and
Christophe Berra with 38 appearances, 12. Holland, 13. 27
14. Guinea, 15. Kevin Bru

PAGE 48
TEST YOURSELF ON 2015, THE CHAMPIONSHIP

1. 28,438 (v West Bromwich Albion, FA Cup 4th round, 24 January 2015),
2. Jordan Rhodes with 21 League goals, 3. Ben Amos, 4. Middlesbrough,
5. True, 6. 99, 7. Sam Vokes, 8. True, 9. Stephen Henderson,
10. Paul Clement, 11. Ross McCormack, 12. Conor Coady with 48
appearances, 13. Sam Clucas, 14. Josh Yorwerth, 15. Neil Redfearn,
16. Brighton & Hove Albion, 17. Dean Lewington, 18. Henri Lansbury,
19. Yellow and blue, 20. Jay Emmanuel-Thomas, 21. Brentford,
22. Danny Ward, 23. Middlesbrough, 24. Silverbug

PAGE 52 · SPOT → THE DIFFERENCE

PAGE 54 · MEGA PIXELS

1. David McGoldrick, 2. Brett Pitman,
3. Adam McDonnell, 4. Daryl Murphy,
5. Tommy Smith, 6. Luke Chambers,
7. Christophe Berra, 8. Giles Coke,
9. Jonas Knudsen

PAGE 59 · PUZZLE IT OUT

CAREER WATCH
2004-2009: Southampton, 2009-2013: Nottingham Forest

WHO ARE YER?
Dean Gerken, Ryan Fraser and Cole Skuse

DERBY DAY
1. Derby County - Nottingham Forest,
2. Brighton & Hove Albion - Crystal Palace,
3. Ipswich Town - Norwich City,
4. Wolverhampton Wanderers - West Bromwich Albion

HOMELANDS
Jonathan Parr - Norway, Kévin Bru - Mauritius,
Daryl Murphy - Republic of Ireland, Bartosz Białkowski - Poland,
Christophe Berra - Scotland, Tommy Smith - New Zealand